This book is an accumulation of inform........ ....
methods people are using to grow Marijuana indoors under artificial
lights. This book is in no way intended to encourage or promote the
illegal cultivation of Marijuana. It is illegal to cultivate Marijuana in
the United States as in most countries, therefore, it is the author's
recommendation that you read this book for your own personal information. However, much of the information in this book can be
applied to growing the majority of legal plants such as most house
plants, vegetables, and many of the tropical plants that under normal
conditions cannot be cultivated in a home.

HOW TO GROW MARIJUANA INDOORS UNDER LIGHTS

by

MURPHY STEVENS

Cover photo by Trebor Worfner

Wholesale inquiries to:
Sun Magic Publishing
911 N.E. 45th Street
Seattle, Washington 98105

TABLE OF CONTENTS

Chapter 1
INTRODUCTION

GROWING MARIJUANA INDOORS

All you have to do to grow Marijuana is to put a seed in the ground, water it, and give it some light. From this book, you will learn how to do these three things in the best possible ways to insure a strong, healthy and productive plant. You will also discover that it is not only fun and interesting to grow plants indoors but practical and easy as well.

If you have a Gro-Lux light or plan on getting one you will also learn how to use it to its best advantage and your plants will grow much more rapidly than those plants grown in natural sunlight or under other types of artificial light. With a Gro-Lux light and the knowledge you are about to receive you can create a perfectly controlled environment for your plants; one in which they will flourish and be plentiful.

Just put your seeds in between about six damp paper towels and put them in a warm place and you are on your way . . .

CHOOSING AND GERMINATING YOUR SEEDS

If you're a seasoned smoker, no doubt you've stashed away super seeds from some dynamite lid, hoping that you could duplicate it. If you haven't, you really should because you will want to use the best seeds you can find.

The quality of the grass you grow is determined mainly by the genetic makeup of the seeds. In other words, the seeds you choose have a potential quality before you do anything to them. You cannot grow a high-grade, potent strain from the seeds of a low-grade marijuana plant. You can, however, provide the best possible soil and growing conditions for your plants so that they will reach their highest possible potency. Improper growing conditions can result in a poor strain of cannabis regardless of how prime the seeds are. The best seeds come from Southeast Asia. These seem to grow faster and are often naturally polyploid. In the marijuana field, polyploid is a good way to be.

eproduced; the fertilized ovule con-
embryo. **2** That from w~~~~~ny-
ngs; source. **3** Offsprin~~~~~en.
le fert~~~~ing ~~~~ement se~~~~milt.
all se~~~~e fr~~~~al~~~~p~~~~f
m which it ma~~~~p~~~~ag~~~~d, as
ers, etc. ~~~~A young oyst~~~~t for
ing. **7** ~~~~ce; gener~~~~tion,~~~~h.
d-bearing stage; he~~~~, over~~~~e-
U.S. Dial. An a~~~~mal or animals
eeding. **—** *v.t.* **1** ~~~~~~~~th seed.
(seed). **3** To remove~~~~~~~~om
isins. **4** In sports: a T~~~~ar~~~~

When your seeds sprout, plant them immediately. If the root is allowed to grow in the paper towel, the seed will suffer when you place it in the soil. This is because the root has hundreds of fine hairs, making it almost impossible to plant without some damage.

It's a good idea to have everything ready to go before you germinate your seed. If your seeds germinate quickly and are ready to go before you are, they won't get planted at the right time. It is very important for your plants to get a good start. If a plant doesn't start growing like crazy from the beginning, it never seems to reach its full growing potential.

It is best if you plant your seed sprout in the soil with the root pointing up, but it isn't essential.

In germinating seeds the most widely used method is to put the seeds in between six moist paper towels. The reason for using six towels is so that they will remain moist until the seeds germinate. If the towels should dry out before germination, the seeds will die. Put the paper towels in a warm, dark part of your house. The seeds will take from twelve hours to one week to germinate. Look at them every day. The seeds that germinate first are usually the strongest, healthiest ones; and they will produce the fastest-growing plants. Unless you are hurting for seeds, throw away the ones that are late starters and germinate another batch, planting only the best sprouts from each.

CHOOSING YOUR SOIL

The soil you use will be a major factor in determining how fast your plants grow and how healthy they will be. Don't fail to use high quality soil (buy it if you have to), you'll be much more pleased with your results.

You will want to use a sandy soil in order to provide good drainage. It should be rich in nutrients and not lacking in any elements. Trace elements are chemicals found in the soil in very small amounts. If they are lacking, your plants will be lacking.

It is also important to use soil that has been sterilized. In sterilized soil you wan't find an assortment of bugs that will eat your plants. There is a fungus in some unsterilized soil that attacks plants when they are only a few days old. The young shoots will fall over and die as a result of this phenomenon called "dampening off".

Your soil should also be loose. To loosen up your soil you can add peat moss, vermiculite, or pumice, (also called "sponge rock"). These will aid in water retention and aeration. If you can, buy a bag of worm castings at a plant shop or a garden supply store. It's pretty expensive, but you'll find that your plants will thrive in soil that has been enriched to contain about 25 percent worm castings. Compared to ordinary soil, these castings contain five times as much nitrogen, seven times as much phosphate and eleven times as much potassium.

A nursery or garden shop will usually have potting soil which is sterile, sandy, rich and loose; but the pH factor of this soil will often be lower than the optimum for Cannabis. The pH refers to the acidity of the soil, and is rated on a scale of 1 to 15. Seven is neutral; any number higher than seven is alkaline and anything lower is acidic. I have come to the conclusion that the best pH for Marijuana is about 6.3 to 7.3.

You will find that the pH of the soil tends to drop into the acidic range after a period of time. Normal watering and fertilizing constantly change the soil. Know the pH of the water you use and monitor the pH of your soil. Try to stabilize the soil within the pH range suggested above.

In most cases, Cannabis will not grow very fast in acidic soil. Common problems of plants grown in acidic soil are the yellowing of the lower leaves and stunted growth. Although both of these symptoms may be the result of any one of many different deficiencies, you may always assume that acidic soil is a contributing factor.

PH soil test kits are available for about $2.75 in most areas. You can also use litmus paper. If you find your soil to be acidic, lime the soil by using hydrated lime, chalk, pulverized limestone, eggshells or limestone screenings. These are listed by speed of release: hydrated lime will raise pH more quickly than the lime screenings, but the effects of the latter will be more long-lasting.

If you save your eggshells, you'll have a ready source of lime. Let the shells dry, then pulverize them in a mortar or an electric blender. Approximately 3 cups will give you a 1.0 increase in one cubic foot of neutral soil. That's about one-half cup of eggshells per gallon of soil. You should bear in mind that eggshells are a relatively slow release source of lime.

If you add peat moss to your soil, remember that it has a pH of approximately 5.4. Always test the soil *after* adding the peat, and then add enough lime to adjust the pH to 7.

"Mica Peat" is a new commercial product on the market. It contains peat moss and vermiculite with trace elements and lime already added. The pH is 7. Mica Peat works very well and it is relatively inexpensive. It comes packaged in large bales like peat moss and costs around $7.50 a bale.

Chapter 2
CONTAINERS

CONTAINER FOR STARTING

After your seeds have sprouted you'll want to plant them in something that will minimize the chances of damaging the root system when transplanting. You can plant them in a flat box of soil or in empty yogurt cartons, but the easiest and best containers to use for starting your seeds are either "Jiffy Pots" or "Jiffy-7" pellets.

A "Jiffy Pot" is a pot made of compressed peat moss. It will hold together remarkably well as long as it is standing out in the air, but when you place it underground the peat moss will gradually decompose so that the roots of the plant can pass right through the walls into the outside soil. The only problems is that the process of decomposition is quite often too slow and the roots get stuck inside the pot, stunting the plant's growth. To make sure this doesn't happen, soak the peat pot in water for a minute to soften it before you lower it into the new container of soil. If the roots of the plant have not yet begun to grow through the walls of the pot, you can just peel the pot off without hurting the roots.

You don't have to remove the Jiffy Pot to repot it.

"Jiffy-7's" are also very good for starting your seeds. The Jiffy-7 is an amazing little pellet of compressed peat moss with nutrients added. The pellet is wrapped in a nylon mesh. When you place this compressed wafer into about an inch of water, it will expand into a little ball of soil held together by the nylon mesh. It takes about five minutes for the pellet to expand to about seven times its original size.

After the Jiffy-7 has expanded, poke a little hole in the top and plant the seed about ¼ inch deep. Plant it with the root pointing up.

As your plant starts to grow, the roots will soon grow through the nylon mesh. This is the time to transplant into a larger container. Simply dig a hole in the soil and place the whole Jiffy-7 in the ground.

Jiffy-7's are really good because you don't have to dig your plant out of its original soil and bother it. Your plant won't even know it's been transplanted and therefore will not be shocked.

If you shock it — you stunt it.

I must add however, that the pH of the Jiffy-7 is a bit acidic. It would definitely be worth while to add lime to the water that you use to expand the Jiffy pellets. Mix it at the rate of ½ cup of lime per gallon of water.

CONTAINERS FOR GROWING UP

When your Jiffy Pots or Jiffy-7's are ready to be transplanted, you will want to acquire some large containers for the plants to mature in. I have found that a three gallon can works fine, and you can normally grow a plant up to seven feet in height if your soil is good and you fertilize regularly. You can usually pick up this size can for practically nothing in bakeries since they throw them away. You can also use two gallon cardboard ice cream cartons.

I've discovered that transplanting plants into large flower boxes or troughs full of dirt is *not* a real fine idea. For one thing, as the plants grow and become bigger, they will get too crowded. They'll have to fight each other for the available light and in doing so will grow straight up and get scrawny. The Gro-Lux lights have to be quite close to the plants to be efficient. If you have several plants in one trough, they may grow at different rates and you'll end up with the tops of some of your plants too far away from the light. Growing each plant in a separate container allows you to make adjustments. As the plants get bushier you can move them farther apart. You can hang your light fixture at an angle and put the shorter plants under the low end of the fixture with the taller ones at the high end. Flower boxes or troughs will also take more soil than individual containers. and it can become expensive if you buy your soil. You'll also find that when you're ready to make a quick change of residence, huge troughs of soil are quite heavy and definitely not as portable as individual containers.

In choosing your containers remember that too small a container will stunt your plant. A container 13 inches deep and about 11 inches in diameter is sufficient, but a larger container would be better.

Chapter 3
YOUR PLANTS' ENVIRONMENT

WATER

How often and how much to water your marijuana plant varies according to the size of the plants, the temperature of the soil, and the amount of light they are getting. Generally, the faster your cannabis is growing, the more water it will use. However, this is not to say that by watering more, your plants will grow faster.

When cannabis plants are small they have a small root system. Therefore, they do not have as great a capability for collecting the available moisture in the soil. You will probably have to water your small plants every day because the roots are small and the small pots dry out faster than larger ones.

As a plant gets larger and is put into a larger pot, the soil won't dry out as fast and the roots will be down deeper where it is usually damp.

A rule of thumb when watering cannabis is: If the soil is damp, don't water; if it is semi-dry, water it. Caution should be taken to make sure that the soil a few inches down is not wet. Very often you will find that the surface soil is dry, but down a few inches where the roots are, the soil is soggy. This can kill the plant because the roots actually drown and rot. If you are unsure about when to water just stick your finger in the pot and feel. Good drainage is essential. You must have holes in the bottom of the container, and a loose enough soil, so that the excess water can drain out and the roots will not be constantly wet.

Use your finger to test your soil for moisture.

Your plants will grow faster if you use slightly warm water when you water.

If you let the water sit for approximately 24 hours before using it on your plants, some of the chlorine in the water will dissipate and your plants will be healthier. Rain water would probably be the best, but it's not too practical.

If the tips of your leaves turn brown, then you are most likely over-watering or your container is not draining properly.

It is best to water about every 3 or 4 days, according to how much the plant is using and how fast it is drying out. It is not a good idea to water a little bit every day, because the water doesn't reach certain areas of the soil. If you give your plant about a pint to a quart of water, the soil will be evenly moist.

TEMPERATURE OF THE AIR

Marijuana can grow in temperatures of 50 degrees F. upwards past 100 degrees F. The ideal daytime temperature however is between 70 degrees F. and 80 degrees F. Plants grow better if the temperature of the air drops about 10 degrees during the dark period.

TEMPERATURE OF SOIL

If your plants are indoors, I wouldn't worry about the temperature of the soil.

If you are growing in a place where it is very cold (below 50 degrees F.) then a soil heating cable would be beneficial. (It will warm the soil to about 70 degrees F.). These cables cost from $6.00 to $10.00 and will plug into any outlet.

FERTILIZERS

Fertilizing is an important aspect of growing marijuana, in fact it is the point where many growers either make it or break it. The common mistake is that a person figures that if a little bit of fertilizer makes his plant grow faster, then more will make it grow faster still. As a result, many people burn their plants. If you follow the directions on the label, everything will be cool and nobody will get burned.

The most widely used fertilizer for cannabis is Ra-Pid-Gro. Ra-Pid-Gro contains a chemical formula of 23-19-17 meaning that it contains 23 percent nitrogen, 19 percent phosphorous, and 17 percent potash. It also contains the following trace elements: potassium, sodium, boron, zinc, sulfur, silicon, calcium, cobalt, iron, chlorine, molybdenum, magnesium, aluminum, manganese, and it contains plant hormones and Vitamins B1 and B2.

A general rule to follow when using fertilizer is to dilute it with more water than the directions say. You can always add more fertilizer, but one overdose and you can harm a whole crop.

Ra-Pid-Gro can be mixed one teaspoon to two quarts of water, but one teaspoon to three quarts is safer, especially if you are leaf-feeding your plants.

Start fertilizing your plants when they are three weeks to a month old, using a high nitrogen fertilizer (such as Ra-Pid-Gro). Nitrogen stimulates stem growth as well as foliage growth. After the plants are about 3½ months old, if you want them to bloom, add a fertilizer low in nitrogen and high in phosphorous and potash. African Violet Blossom Booster contains a formula of 4-10-10, which means it contains 4 percent nitrogen, 10 percent phosphorous, and 10 percent potash. This fertilizer will encourage your plants to bloom with little stem and foliage growth.

Leaf-feeding is a very effective method of fertilizing plants. This method employs a spray bottle, and the fertilizer is sprayed directly on the foliage rather than being added to the soil. Spray the mixture on, misting the leaves thoroughly. Be careful not to saturate the leaves of plants that are under a foot high since they can't take the fertilizer when they are small. The weight of solution on the leaves can topple a plant if applied too thick on a small plant. Leaf feeding should be done in the evening to obtain maximum efficiency in absorbtion of the food. The advantage of leaf-feeding is that more fertilizer is absorbed through the leaves at a faster rate than with root feeding. Also, by adding fertilizer to the soil, you make the soil more acidic and build up the salt content. If the salt content in the soil reaches a certain level it can stunt your plants.

The Ra-Pid-Gro company claims that up to 95 percent of the fertilizer you spray on the leaves is absorbed. You can fertilize your plants about once a week. Caution should be taken in fertilizing plants that are under three weeks old, since they are rather tender and will burn quite easily.

WORMS

One of the true joys of growing your own is in being able to go to a completely organic system of cultivation. The scientific methods of fertilizing will satisfy most of the people reading this book. It is for those of you who wish to avoid the use of chemicals that the following paragraphs are dedicated.

The best friend of the organic gardener is the earthworm. That juicy night crawler that's loved by fish and fowl is also much appreciated by the plant kingdom. Aristotle called them "the intestines of the earth" because as they pass through the soil, they digest and condition it. Their tunnels, sometimes reaching depths of six feet or more, are lined with minerally rich worm castings. These tunnels aerate the soil, promote the growth of the valuable bacteria and make it easy for air to reach the roots. Rain also courses through these tunnels, dissolving the rich worm castings and providing the best possible food for your plants.

Earthworms thrive on organic matter and the organic gardener shouldn't use any other fertilizers. Chemical fertilizers are fatal to worms because they will create acidic conditions in your soil.

For the organic grower, Alaska fish fertilizer is quite effective and this too can be applied by spraying on the leaves. It gets a little smelly, but it is worth the added growth. The fertilizer should be mixed at the rate of one teaspoon per 1½ gallons of water for leaf-feeding. If you apply the mixture to the ground you can mix 1 tablespoon of fish fertilizer to one gallon of water.

Fish fertilizer is a bit smelly, but the added growth is worth it.

BUGS, ANIMALS AND DISEASE

Just about every animal loves cannabis. You will find that you are often plagued with animals, insects, and disease if you are growing outdoors.

Out in the wilds you will find that deer, rabbits, squirrels, bears, and all their friends will take it upon themselves to get off on your weed at any opportunity. In your neighborhood you'll find slugs, aphids, spider mites, and an assortment of other pests, including your fellow neighborhood hippy, who will sometimes rip you off without considering the many hours of work you have put into your plants, nor the affection that you have acquired for them.

A WORD TO THE POTENTIAL RIP-OFF MAN: Instead of pulling up whole cannabis plants by their roots, cut off only the tops. If you leave the main stalk intact with just one set of leaves, new branches will grow out and the owner can at least enjoy a partial harvest.

Getting back to bugs and things, you will find that pests of some sort will try to get to your plants even if you have them indoors. The worst pests in the northwest part of the United States are spider mites and white flies. The spider mite is almost too small to see without a magnifying glass, but you will notice its silvery webbing on the plant before you find the leaves turning a dull whitish-gray color and then browning. The plant often ceases to grow completely. White flies spread rapidly, and they have to be sprayed repeatedly with insecticides to be destroyed. The same holds true for spider mites. When using an insecticide, you will want to choose one that will break down and not kill you after it kills the bugs. Diazinon will work for killing most bugs, and it is relatively safe since it breaks down in two or three days. If Diazinon does not work, you will have to use Malathion, which breaks down in about seven days.

Aphids are also a common problem indoors. An effective method of ridding your plants of Aphids is to employ our friend, the ladybug, who will eat ten times her weight in bugs a day.

In the wilds, you will find that blood meal sprinkled around the ground will keep the deer from feasting on your grass.

Powdery mildew is a fungus disease which appears as a white or gray powder or mealy coating on the leaves. Plants are most susceptible under conditions of high humidity, crowding of plants, poor air circulation and lack of light. Dusting your plants with sulfur will eliminate powdery mildew. Sulfur may be obtained at any garden center. Be careful not to confuse powdery mildew with spider mites. Mites are a far more common problem and will do far greater damage to your plants.

Chapter 4
GROWING INDOORS WITH LIGHTS

GRO-LUX LIGHTS

Gro-Lux lights are fluorescent lights that emit high concentrations of red and blue bands of the light spectrum. These are the main colors that plants use for photosynthesis. Gro-Lux lights come in all sizes, from 12 inches to 8 feet, and fit standard fluorescent fixtures.

With Gro-Lux lights, you can grow plants in your basement, closet, or attic at nearly the same rate as those plants growing outdoors in the height of summer. The quality of home-grown grass is far superior to the average Mexican lid. The nice thing about growing indoors is that you can control the plant's environment completely, and you're not as likely to be troubled with previously mentioned pests.

TYPES OF GRO-LUX LIGHTS

There are two basic types of Gro-Lux lights: the Standard Gro-Lux and the Gro-Lux Wide Spectrum. The Standard Gro-Lux light is better than the wide spectrum, because it emits more red and blue light. Not only does the wide spectrum emit less red and blue light than the Standard, but it also puts off more infra-red light. Infra-red light is undesirable to seedlings because it promotes rapid stem growth. If you are using only Wide-Spectrum lights, you'll find that your plants are growing tall and spindly. The Wide-Spectrum lamp was developed for use as a supplementary source of lighting, such as that needed in a greenhouse.

Both the wide spectrum and Standard Gro-Lux lights come in three intensities: "regular output," "high output," and "very high output" (VHO). All together there are six types of Gro-Lux lamps; two for each intensity. The VHO fixture and lamp units are superior by far to the others.

There are other fluorescent lamps which are beneficial to plant growth besides the Gro-Lux lamps. The regular Cool White fluorescent lamps found in most buildings work quite well when used in conjunction with Gro-Lux lamps. The Cool White (CW) lamp emits about the same amount of blue light as the Standard Gro-Lux, but it is lacking in the red area of the light spectrum. The Cool White lamp emits only 9 percent red light while the Standard Gro-Lux emits 39 percent. The reason that the two lamps work well together is that the plants will receive sufficient red light from the Gro-Lux for stem growth, and the additional blue light emitted from the Cool White will stimulate foliage growth. You will probably find, however, that two Standard Gro-Lux lights work even better.

There are other companies which manufacture lights which promote growth in plants. These are marketed under such trade names as "Vita-Lite," "Naturescent," and "Dura-Lite." Each of these companies will make claims for their products. My advice is to make your own judgment based on the output of the lights, remembering that plants basically need red and blue light.

An incandescent light (regular light bulb) emits high amounts of red light, so using a combination of Cool White lamps and Incandescent lamps will give you a pretty good combination of red and blue light. One drawback, however, of using incandescent lamps is that they emit a high percentage of infra-red light which will cause excessive stem growth, especially in the early stages. If you already have Cool White lamps and sockets for incandescent lights, then you can save yourself some money by using this combination of lighting and still successfully grow plants indoors. If you don't have anything

26

and have to buy all your equipment before you start, don't hassle with the Cool White and incandescent lights. They will probably end up costing you as much as Gro-Lux units would, and are more of a problem when it comes time to raise the lights to allow for plant growth.

Below is a graph comparing the percentages of light emitted in each color band of the spectrum by the Standard Gro-Lux, the Wide Spectrum Gro-Lux, Cool White, and daylight.

ENERGY EMISSION IN ARBITRARY COLOR BANDS
40 WATT FLUORESCENT LAMPS
In Watts and Percent of Total Emission

	Band in Nano-meters	Daylight		Cool White		Std Gro-Lux		Gro-Lux/ws	
		Watts	Percent	Watts	Percent	Watts	Percent	Watts	Percent
Ultra-Violet	-380	0.186	2.15	0.16	1.68	0.10	1.42	0.27	3.16
Violet	380-430	0.832	9.60	0.72	7.57	0.70	9.67	1.07	12.48
Blue	430-490	2.418	27.91	1.98	20.78	1.96	27.07	1.22	14.29
Green	490-560	2.372	27.38	2.35	24.67	1.02	14.02	1.24	14.49
Yellow	560-590	1.259	14.53	1.74	18.27	0.10	1.42	0.83	9.77
Orange	590-630	1.144	13.21	1.69	17.75	0.44	6.05	1.36	15.93
Red	630-700	0.452	5.22	0.81	8.47	2.86	39.55	1.86	21.78
Far-Red	700-780	0.13	1.53	0.07	0.81	0.06	0.80	0.69	8.10
TOTAL		8.89	100.00	9.52	100.00	7.24	100.00	8.54	100.00

The life expectency of a four foot Gro-Lux lamp according to Sylvania is 18,000 hours. A regular output eight foot Gro-Lux lamp is supposed to last 12,000 hours and a VHO Gro-Lux lamp is rated at 9,000 hours.

Gro-Lux lights use little electricity compared to a regular 100 watt light bulb. The 4 foot Gro-Lux lamp uses 40 watts of electricity and the 8 foot Gro-Lux light uses 73 watts. The 8 foot VHO Gro-Lux light uses 215 watts.

The cost of operating an 8 foot fixture with two 8 foot Gro-Lux lights in it is around $2.00 per month.

HIGH OUTPUT AND VERY HIGH OUTPUT LIGHTS

HO and VHO Gro-Lux lights emit higher intensities of light which result in the faster growth of your plants.

The High Output (HO) lamp emits 1½ times more intensity. It is a very efficient lamp and excellent results can be obtained from it. In order to use an HO Gro-Lux lamp you must also have a High Output fluorescent fixture in which to house it.

A Very High Output Gro-Lux lamp is the top of the line. The rate plants grow under these lights is amazing. They cost quite a bit more but are worth it. Here again you must use a VHO fluorescent fixture with VHO lamps and the fixture is the main cost. Often you can find a used VHO fixture in a junk yard for little money. The cost of a new VHO Fluorescent fixture is about $60.00 and the price of each VHO Gro-Lux lamp is about $10.00

HOW TO USE GRO-LUX LIGHTS

When using Gro-Lux lights the single most important factor to keep in mind is to position the lamps very close to the tops of your plants. This means, of course, that when your plants start growing fast, you will have to raise the lights quite often.

According to Sylvania's instructions, Gro-Lux lights should be kept from 8 to 18 inches from the plants. I must stress to you, however, that Sylvania is in the lighting business, not in the plant business. Gro-Lux lamps should be kept about two-inches from the top of the plants and as close as one inch from seedlings. The reasoning being that the intensity of the light is reduced greatly as it gets further away. If the light is a foot or two from the plants, they strain to reach the area of higher intensity light. As a result, the plants get a long stem with very few leaves. If this occurs, you can prop your plant up with a toothpick and wait for it to get a stronger stem, or, if your plant has a few sets of leaves, you can trim it down to take some of the weight off the top. This will also encourage your plant to become bushy while giving the stem a chance to gain some strength. (Refer to section on "Pruning your Plants"). You can also transplant the small plant to a larger container, setting it deeper into the soil so that the soil level is higher up on the stalk, providing more support.

Roots will start growing out of the stalk that has been covered with soil. The new larger root system will result in a stronger, healthier plant.

It is possible that your plant may acquire stem rot, which simply means that the bacteria in the soil will act on the tissues in the newly covered stem causing it to rot. Using sterilized soil will probably alleviate this problem. You can sterilize your soil by putting it in the oven for about an hour at 150 degrees F.

THE AMOUNT OF LIGHT AND THE RATE OF GROWTH

The more light you give cannabis the faster it will grow. Therefore, two lamps placed next to each other are more effective than one. A plant will grow under a single lamp, but the intensity of light will not be great enough to produce a strong, bushy plant. Using only one lamp will cause the same problems that are created by keeping the lamps too far from the plants. Again, the seedlings will "stretch" to get close to the lamp where the high intensity light is and will soon become spindly. Two or more lamps produce a high enough intensity of light to assure strong, leafy, fast-growing specimens.

High Output and Very High Output lamps emit a lot more light than regular output lamps. The growth rate of cannabis under VHO lamps is really unbelievable. Provided with proper conditions, (good soil, large container, adequate water), you can grow a plant to a height of four feet in two months.

THE LENGTH OF LIGHT PER DAY

The length of time you keep your lights on per day will have a great effect on your plants. It will determine the rate at which they grow and also the length of time it will take them to mature and flower. In order for your plants to flower you must allow them a dark period in each 24 hour cycle.

If you want your plant to produce seeds for your next crop or to develop hybrid strains, then allow your plant a dark period each day. If, on the other hand, you are more interested in a constant supply of foliage, then leave your lights on 24 hours a day. Contrary to what you learned in your Botany class, this constant exposure to light will not harm your plants.

When Cannabis blooms, the amount of resin in the plant increases, improving the quality of the grass. However, a plant also gets more resinous and of a higher quality as it grows older. A three month old plant that hasn't bloomed is better than a two month old plant that has bloomed. The three month old plant has a lot more leaves besides.

It is to your advantage to keep your plants from blooming, at least until your plants are 6 months old. The blossoms are, of course, the most potent portion of the plant; but the blossoms taken from a six month old plant are far more potent than they would have been had you encouraged you plant to bloom at three months. So, if you want your plants to bloom, after six or eight months of constant light, start allowing them a dark period each day.

The following is a breakdown of the number of hours of light given each day and the effect it has on the plants:

With 12 hours of light a day plants will flower in about 2 to 2½ months.

With 16 hours of light a day plants will flower in about 3½ to 4 months.

With 18 hours of light a day plants will flower in about 4½ to 5 months.

ARRANGING YOUR LIGHTS
FOR MAXIMUM EFFICIENCY

If you have more than one fluorescent fixture, you should arrange them so as to obtain maximum amount of light per plant.

Two fixtures should run parallel and as close to each other as possible, leaving enough room for the pots and for the plants to grow. Two rows of plants should then be arranged under these two fixtures.

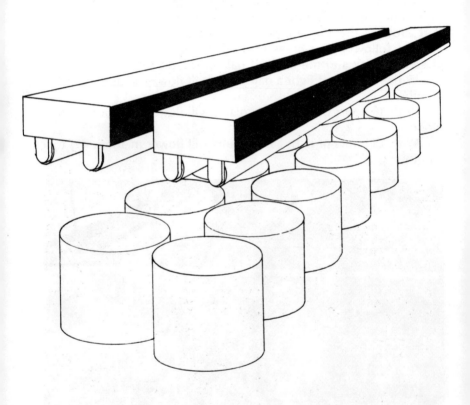

With the lights close together, both rows of plants will benefit from all the lights. Be sure to have each row directly under each fixture. If your plants are off to the side of the light, they will grow at an angle toward the light. This will entually cause the plants to get top-heavy and fall over.

If you wish to do so, you may put a third row of plants in between the original two rows of plants and lights. This middle row will not be directly under any light, but will benefit from the lights on each side. The plants in the middle row will have to be moved as they get bigger so they don't crowd the plants in the other two rows. However, when these plants get so big that they're crowding the other plants, you can always harvest them, and even if they're only two feet high they will still give you a nice stash to tide you over until your other plants are ready. If you're like most people, you won't have the heart to pull them up at this stage. They will have reached a point where they will start growing faster and you'll probably end up buying another set of lights to keep them going. It is easier to become addicted to growing than it is to smoking.

At the end of this book, starting on page 66, is an appendix that goes into some detail on the technical aspects of hanging and mounting your Gro-Lux light fixtures. You might find it helpful to refer to that appendix when setting up an indoor growing area.

MARIJUANA LEAF: This close-up photograph shows some very interesting detail of a leaf taken from a marijuana plant of Afghanistani stock. I am uncertain as to the nature of the golden brown coloration, but I'm pretty sure that it is not from any mineral dificiency. It could be a burn from too much fertilizer, but that type of problem generally shows up at the tips of the leaves and not at the base. Frankly I'm not sure what it is.

VENTILATION IN YOUR ROOM

Proper ventilation in your growing room is fairly important. The more plants you have in one room, the more important good ventilation becomes.

Plants breathe through their leaves. They also rid themselves of poisons through their leaves. If proper ventilation is not maintained, the pores of the leaves will become clogged and the leaves will die. If there is a free movement of air, the poisons can evaporate off the leaves, and the plant can breathe and remain healthy.

In a small closet where there are only a few plants, you can probably create enough air circulation just by opening the door to look at them. Although it is possible to grow healthy looking plants in poorly ventilated rooms, they would be larger and even healthier if they had a fresh supply of air coming in.

In a small growing room you can create enough circulation by opening the door for a look.

If you spend a lot of time in your growing room, your plants will grow better because they will be using the carbon dioxide that you are exhaling around them.

It is sometimes quite difficult to get a fresh supply of air into your growing room because your room is usually hidden away in a secret corner of your house, possibly in the attic or basement. In this case, a fan will create some movement of air. It will also stimulate your plants into growing a healthier and sturdier stalk. Often times in an indoor environment, the stems of plants fail to become rigid because they don't have to cope with elements of wind and rain. To a degree, though, this is an advantage because the plant puts most of its energy into producing leaves and resin instead of stems.

DEHUMIDIFYING YOUR GROWING ROOM

Cannabis that grows in a hot, dry climate will have narrower leaves than cannabis grown in a humid atmosphere. The reason is that in a dry atmosphere the plant can respirate easier because the moisture on the leaves evaporates faster. In a humid atmosphere the moisture cannot evaporate as fast. Consequently, the leaves have to be broader, with more sufrace area, in order to expel the wastes that the plant puts off. Since the broad leaves produce less resin per leaf than the narrow leaves, there will be more resin in an ounce of narrow leaves than in an ounce of broad leaves. There may be more leaf mass in the broader leafed plants, but most people are growing their own for quality rather than quantity.

Since the resin in the marijuana plant serves the purpose of keeping the leaves from drying out, there is more apt to be a lot of resin produced in a dry room than in a humid one.

In the "Sears" catalog dehumidifiers cost around $100.00 and so are a bit impractical for the "Hobby Grower".

Above: Home-grown Thai weed.
Left: Home-grown Afghanistan weed.

Notice the difference in the width of the leaves between this specimen and the afghani plant on page 36. Both these plants were grown by the author under identical conditions in an upstairs bedroom.

PRUNING YOUR PLANTS

You can increase foliage production if you prune your plants. Clipping will encourage secondary growth and allow light to reach the less mature leaves.

You should prune your plants for the first time when they are three weeks old. Cut the top of the plant, severing the stalk just above one of the leaf clusters.

These clippings can be dried and smoked as the first rewards of your labors. Don't expect more than a little buzz however. The plants are still young and have not had time to reach a mature state of high potency.

When you prune off the tops of your plants the secondary growth above each leaf will be stimulated and will grow into almost stalklike branches themselves. Many leaf clusters will grow out of these branches and more branches will grow above each leaf.

By pruning your plants you can get them to grow bushy rather than tall and spindly. When the secondary branches get at least four sets of leaves, it is time to prune them just as you did the main stalk the first time you trimmed. Out of each of the four leaves you left on the secondary branch, four new secondary branches will be stimulated to grow and so on. Clip the new secondary branches about every ten days.

You may also trim off main leaf clusters to promote secondary growth. Taking off some of the big leaves will allow more light to reach the branches underneath them. The top leaves of each branch are the best and so by stimulating more branches to grow, you will have more top leaves.

As the plants grow you can continue pruning them in this fashion. The clippings will provide you with a constant stash and at the same time, your plant will be producing more and more leaves. The quality of the plant also increases as the plant gets older. You'll just get more and more and it will get better and better.

The author testing for quality.

Chapter 5
IF YOUR PLANTS
ARE NOT FEELING UP TO PAR

It is difficult to single out one particular reason why a plant is not growing as fast as its friends, or why it is doing certain weird things; but there are a few signs that can be easily diagnosed.

Tips of the Leaves Turning Brown

This is either the result of overwatering or poor drainage. Either punch more holes in the bottom of your container or cut down on the water. A good way to tell if the soil needs water is to stick the eraser end of a pencil down about five inches where the roots of the plant are, and see if the eraser is muddy. If it is, you are obviously overwatering. If you are using a sandy soil, you probably won't have this problem because the sand enables the water to run through the soil more freely. Putting about an inch of pebbles in the bottom of the container is a good way to assure proper drainage and alleviate the problem of overwatering.

Plant is Growing Extremely Slow

This can be caused by many things including temperatures below 50 degrees F., lack of adequate light, and poor soil conditions. If the soil doesn't have much humus content, it may become packed after many waterings, inhibiting growth of the root system. If the pH of the soil is below 5, your plants won't grow very well. If the salt content is high, your plants will be stunted. It's a little difficult to ascertain the salt level yourself, but you can have your soil tested for about $3.00 at most agricultural colleges.

Yellowing of Older Leaves

This can be caused by any of the following:
1. A shortage of nitrogen.
2. pH factor too low (acidic).
3. Iron deficiency.
4. Potassium deficiency — if you also get grayish brown spots on edges of leaves.
5. Magnesium deficiency — if there is a yellowing around the veins at first.

Top Leaves Twisted

This is caused by a molybdenum deficiency.
If you suspect a deficiency in the soil, it is a fairly safe bet to spray a mixture of "Ra-Pid-Gro" and water on the leaves of your plants. Mix one teaspoon per two quarts of water.

Plants are Tall and Spindly, Possibly Falling Over

The most likely reason is that the lights are too far away from the top of your plants. They should be only an inch or two away when the plants are small.

This could also be the result of using only one Gro-Lux lamp. If you put two lamps next to each other the plants usually won't do this.

Infra-red light stimulates stem growth. You shouldn't use a heat lamp (which is mainly infra-red light) or a regular light bulb (which emits high amounts of far red light). The Gro-Lux Wide Spectrum lamp emits 10 percent infra-red light. Using wide spectrum lamps alone will tend to make the plants tall and spindly. If you use a Standard Gro-Lux and a Gro-Lux Wide Spectrum together, you should not have any problem with stems that grow too tall.

Too much nitrogen in the soil will stimulate stem growth. Don't fertilize your plants when they are small.

If your pot is too small for the roots to get adequate food from the soil, the plant will grow tall but without many leaves. To remedy this situation, repot your plants in larger containers using sterilized soil. Place the plant further down in the container so that the level of the soil is higher up on the stalk. Roots will soon start growing out of the part of the stem that was previously above the soil level.

Leaves Have a Silvery Webbing Followed by a Whitish Substance

This is caused by spider mites. Spider mites are extremely small and are hard to see without a magnifying glass. At first you only see the webs they make but you will soon see the damage that they do. They suck juices out of the plant, and, after a while, the leaves look like they have a whitish fungus growing on them. The leaves will begin to die and the plant will cease to grow.

These bugs are very difficult to get rid of. I would suggest using Malathion. It is effective and it oxidizes totally within seven days, leaving no lingering residue which might harm you.

Applications should be made every three days over a nine day period. Malathion kills the mites but not their larvae, so you must repeat applications until all the larvae have hatched and have been knocked off.

There are many organic methods for pest control, but I do not presently know of any effective organic methods for killing spider mites.

Chapter 6
IS IT A BOY OR A GIRL?

Male plant showing downward hanging flower petals and pollen sacs.

Female plant showing seed pods with upward pointing pistils.

Determining whether a cannabis plant is male or female is just about impossible in the early stages, because the plant produces no identifiable sex characteristics until it matures. As it reaches maturity, the male plant produces downward hanging white flowers which become heavy with yellow pollen. The female plant matures about two weeks later, exhibiting seed pods with upward pointing pistils. These pistils catch the male pollen, thus fertilizing the seeds.

HERMAPHRODITIC MARIJUANA: Notice the yellow male flower on the same stalk with the female seed pods.

48

Above: Male
Below: Female

Chapter 7
TWO WEEKS BEFORE HARVESTING

One of the reasons that the cannabis plant produces resins is to keep the leaves from drying out in hot weather. This fact can be used to your advantage if you regulate the conditions of your growing room accordingly.

For the two weeks prior to your final harvest, do not water or fertilize your plants. This will start the movement of resins to the leaves to protect them against the loss of too much moisture. Raise the temperature of your growing room and try to keep the humidity down. If you place a sun lamp directly over your plants, the ultra-violet rays and high heat will cause even more resin to flow to the aid of the leaves. You can actually witness the effects of this treatment: the leaves become shiny with resin and are sticky to the touch. The higher the resin content, the higher the quality of your harvest.

You may want to use a limited version of the above procedure for your bi-weekly prunings. Water your plants and fertilize them after a pruning session and not immediately beforehand.

HARVESTING YOUR PLANTS AND CURING YOUR STASH

If you follow the procedures outlined in the last section your plants will be quite resinous. The leaves will be drooping and your well-nurtured marijuana plants will be ready to fulfill their mission in life.

There are a few different ways to cure your crop after harvesting. You can use a drying box, such as is described in "The Cultivator's Handbook of Marijuana" by Bill Drake; or you can try the "Jar" method. This gives satisfactory results without too much hassle.

First, pull off all the leaves and separate them from the stalk. Then put them in a large paper bag, leaving the top of the bag open. Let the grass stay in the bag for three or four days, depending on how many leaves are in the bag. After a few days when the leaves are dry to the touch, but still pliable when you pick them up, transfer them to a jar with a tight fitting lid. At this point, it is imperative that you keep a watchful eye on the grass, because if it is still too wet it will mold in the jar. Open the jar every day to let the moisture out, and smell the grass to make sure that no mold has started. Mold smells really lousy — you'll be able to sniff it out right away. If the grass is molding, take it out of the jar and lay it out on a table so that it can dry quickly. By drying the grass in a closed jar, it will dry very slowly and will acquire the texture of cured tobacco. It will be dry, yet feel semi-moist like tobacco.

Chapter 8
ADDITIONAL IDEAS FOR THE CONNOISSEUR

THE LEVEL OF CO2 AND PLANT GROWTH

In recent years, plant physiologists have found that there is a tremendous increase in plant growth when the amount of carbon dioxide is increased in the growing area. There is still much research being conducted, but in some experiments done on house plants and vegetables, the rate of growth and the size of leaves has been doubled with increased amounts of carbon dioxide. According to a noted botanist (who shall remain nameless because of the nature of this book) a cucumber was edible *six weeks* after it germinated when additional carbon dioxide was used in the growing room.

I've seen pictures of plants grown with increased amounts of CO2 beside pictures of control plants grown in the same environment without the additional CO2 and the difference is unbelievable. The plants that were exposed to the increased amounts of CO2 had at least four times as many leaves as the others, and were blooming while the others were still small seedlings.

There are various methods of adding carbon dioxide to a room. You can get dry ice and let it melt in the room, but this is quite expensive.

You can also obtain tanks of compressed carbon dioxide at welding supply houses. These are quite inexpensive. You can rent a large tank of CO2 for about $10.00 and a $40.00 deposit.

The carbon dioxide should be added during the daytime, or when the lights are on. The level of carbon dioxide should be reduced at night.

The CO2 level should be maintained at about 5 percent. *Be very careful* when using carbon dioxide. If you are in the room and the level of CO2 gets too high, you will die. If you're using a tank, be sure the gas is turned off entirely when not in use.

There are meters available which measure the CO2 level. There are also a couple of different methods of testing the CO2 level without the use of a meter, but they require a certain amount of chemistry.

TREATING MARIJUANA WITH DRY ICE

Marijuana contains both Cannabinol and Tetrahydracannabinol (THC) molecules. The basic difference between them is that the Cannabinol molecule contains one less atom of Carbon than does the THC molecule. Frozen CO2 gives up a Carbon atom and the Cannabinol molecule takes it, thus changing the molecular structure of Cannabinol to that of Tetrahydracannabinol (THC).

The procedure for improving your grass with dry ice is quite simple. Get a ten pound chunk of dry ice and put it in a styrofoam ice chest. (It costs about 20 cents a pound). Put your Marijuana on top of the ice and wrap the ice and the grass up in newspaper or something so that it won't melt too fast. If the styrofoam cooler is small enough and if your freezer is big enough, put one inside of the other.

Leave the grass on ice till it is gone. (The ice, not the grass). The general consensus is that it is best if the grass is left on dry ice for about eight days and 48 hours is the minimum.

It doesn't seem to make much difference if the grass is freshly harvested or old stuff. There is a noticeable difference in quality change when treating poor quality grass than there is when treating grass that is already good. Good grass already has more THC and less Cannabinol. The THC you create by treating with dry ice seems to be unstable and you may find that the weed reverts back to its previous state after a period of time.

TREATING YOUR PLANTS WITH COLCHICINE

Colchicine is a chemical that changes the chromosomal structure of plants. It causes plants to mutate by stopping cell division at a point in the mitosis process just after the cell divides. In order for the plant to sruvive after this stoppage of cell division it must mutate, which results in the plant having twice as many sets of chromosomes.

The end result is a plant which is far more potent. The plants that do survive the ordeal and mutate, sometimes grow very oddly. They often have leaves that are deformed. The leaves are greener and after they get growing they will grow faster and bushier.

You will find that the number of leaves per cluster will be higher than usual. I have seen as many as 17 leaves on one leaf cluster.

Ordinarily, when growing cannabis you will find that the first set of serrated leaves following the primary leaves or "cotyledons" will have just one leaf on each side of the stem.

The next set usually has three leaves on a cluster. When you treat your seeds with colchicine, the second set of serrated leaves will often have five leaves per cluster instead of three.

Colchicine is used in the treatment of Gout. It is a prescription drug, although it sometimes can be purchased from a chemical supply house. Many nurseries use it for developing new strains of plants.

Often times colchicine will cause your leaves to grow rather weirdly.

"Colchicum Major" is a plant sometimes called "Winter Crocus" which is grown from a large bulb. This bulb contains .3 percent Colchicine. You can extract the colchicine from the colchicum bulb by squeezing the liquid out with a garlic press. This liquid should then be filtered through filter paper. (A coffee filter paper is usually a handy one). You will now have a solution with approximately .3 percent colchicine. Mix this solution with an equal part of water. This will reduce the colchicine solution to .15 percent. This is a workable solution for causing plant mutations.

No doubt the percentage of colchicine varies from bulb to bulb, so if you don't think that your plants have responded to the colchicine treatment, you might try using the solution just as is when squeezed from the bulb.

Since colchicine is hard on the seeds, often times many of them will not survive.

Normally you soak your seeds for 24 hours in the solution, but for poor seeds you may want to experiment by taking some of them out after eight hours and some after twelve hours so that some will have a better chance of surviving.

When you take the seeds out of the solution, rinse them lightly and put them in between damp paper towels. Keep them in a warm place, (90 degrees F. is ideal) until they sprout. As soon as a sprout appears, plant the seed immediately.

In "The Cultivator's Handbook of Marijuana", Bill Drake states that you shouldn't smoke the first generation plants that have been treated with colchicine because of the danger of being poisoned. Colchicine is an extremely poisonous chemical; 7.0 mg being considered the lethal dose for humans.

But despite the possible danger, people who have smoked the first generation plants are still alive and happy. Perhaps they have started the beginning of some dread disease which has yet to show itself, but nevertheless, there are living people around who have been smoking first generation cochicine treated grass for at least two years.

People who have gout take one colchicine pill every day. I would think that a plant that had its seed soaked in a .15 percent solution of colchicine would not have very much colchicine in its leaves when it reached a height of six feet. Also smoking the grass would lower the small amount that is in the plant.

I don't, however, want to be responsible for your getting sick, so make up your own mind. My bet is that you're not going to throw a potent six foot marijuana plant in the fireplace.

GROWING CANNABIS OUTDOORS

You may want to grow your marijuana outdoors from the start, or transplant some plants outside that you have started indoors.

When moving plants outdoors, some precautions should be taken.

For one thing, your plants, indoors, have had a pretty easy life. They have not had to deal with the elements of wind, rain, cold and harsh sun. Under Gro-Lux lights they have been exposed to very little ultra violet light so they have not learned to tolerate it. If you move your plants outside on a hot day they will shrivel up in about an hour. Move them when the sun is not too high in the sky, preferably in the evening. If your plants don't have a very strong stem, you should stake them up.

It is a good idea to "harden" your plants before transplanting. Put them outside for about a half hour the first day and bring them back in. The next day leave them out for a longer period of time. Increase the length of time each day for about a week to assure your plants' survival once they are moved outdoors permanently.

Another hazard in transplanting outdoors is the change in soil. In Western Washington and Oregon, the pH factor of the soil is acidic. Chances are you will have been using neutral or alkaline soil indoors, so you should try to find the same type of soil outdoors to avoid shocking your plants. Where there are pine trees, you can bet that the soil is acidic.

You really should test the soil for pH before transplanting and make adjustments if necessary. (Refer to "Choosing your Soil").

Soil that is on the acid side produces mostly male plants that will grow slowly.

THINGS TO REMEMBER

Water from the tap contains some chlorine. The amount of chlorine in tap water varies from place to place. Since chlorine is harmful to plants, it is a good idea to rid the water of as much chlorine as possible before using it. By letting the water sit in a container for at least 24 hours, much of the chlorine will dissipate. Using distilled water is very expensive and catching rain water is a slow and tedious task. You should also use slightly warm rather than cold water on your plants.

Clean air is beneficial to the growth rate and overall health of your plants. No plants like smoke. If you live on a busy street your plants won't get off on the carbon monoxide fumes from cars.

Placing aluminum foil on the walls next to your plants will increase the amount of light that they receive. Make sure that the aluminum foil is placed so that the light is reflected onto the plants. Foil reflects 93 percent of the light that hits it. Placing additional foil on the floor underneath the pots will reflect the light back up onto the under side of the leaves. The underside of the leaves can utilize the light as well as the tops.

Be cautious in fertilizing your plants before they are three weeks old. If you are bent on fertilizing before they reach this age, dilute the fertilizer more than the directions say.

Chapter 9

PLANTING BY THE MOON

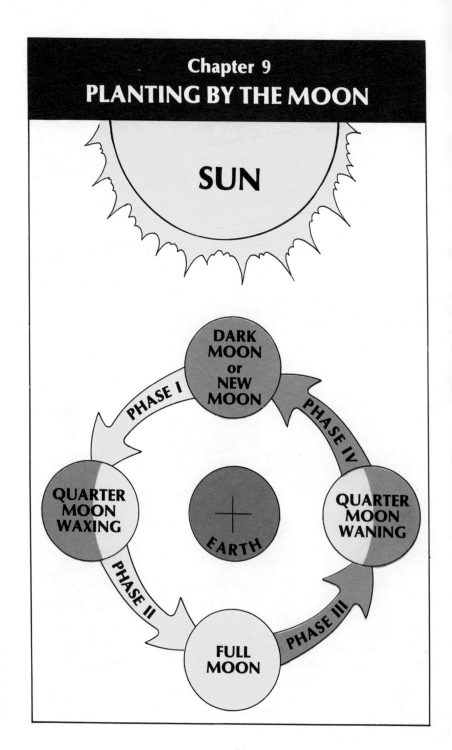

SUN

DARK MOON or NEW MOON

PHASE I

PHASE IV

QUARTER MOON WAXING

EARTH

QUARTER MOON WANING

PHASE II

PHASE III

FULL MOON

The influence of the phases of the moon on the planting and harvesting of crops has been studied since prehistoric times. Monuments like Stonehenge and ancient calendars such as those discovered in South America indicate that men have taken advantage of the effects of the moon and planets for many centuries. The "Old Farmer's Almanac" is evidence of the attention being paid to these forces in 20th century agriculture.

It takes the moon 28 to 29 days to complete one orbit around the earth. This orbit is divided into four phases. It starts as the "new moon" and grow larger, becoming the "quarter moon" and then reaching maturity as the "full moon." At this point, the moon begins to wane, passing through another "quarter moon" and finally becoming the "dark (new) moon" and beginning the cycle again.

Generally speaking, the time for planting is during the period of the waxing (growing) moon. This will be the first half of the moon's monthly cycle, that period when the moon is growing. The second half of the cycle, the waning moon, is best for harvesting. The only days to avoid are the exact days of the quarter moon: these are the days when the Sun and Moon are at a 90-degree angle to each other. This square angle makes for extreme resistance and frustration. The exact day of the new moon and the full moon are also to be avoided. You will notice that on these days, the Sun and Moon are in exact alignment and severe tension is created.

You should plant, germinate, graft and take starts during Phase I and Phase II avoiding, of course, the exact days of the quarter, new and full moon. The best time to go at these tasks is roughly two to three days before the Full Moon, as this period is the most sensitive.

Phases III and IV are best for harvesting, transplanting, pruning and bug killing (again, avoiding the exact days as above). The most sensitive times are two to three days before the Dark Moon. Roots are ruled by this moon and will take better hold if transplanted during this period. It is also important to harvest during the Dark Moon so that your crop will dry better, keep longer and have less tendency to rot.

Appendix A
HANGING AND MOUNTING
YOUR FIXTURES

Mounting your Gro-Lux unit is very simple. There are a variety of ways in which you may do it. One of the easiest ways is to screw a hook into the ceiling and run a rope around it with one end tied to the fixture and the other end tied to something that will support its weight.

You can adjust the height of the lights as the plants grow by taking up the rope more and re-tying it. If possible, screw the ceiling

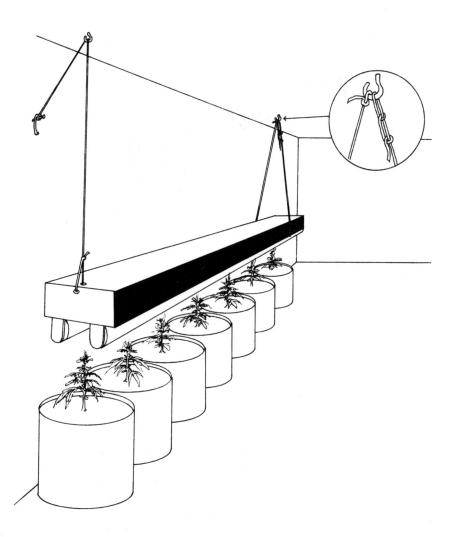

hook into a stud to be sure it will hold the weight of the fixture. If you can't find a stud, then you can use a "Molly Bolt". You must first drill a hole in the ceiling and then insert the molly bolt into the hole. When it goes in far enough, the flanges will pop open and the hook is secure.

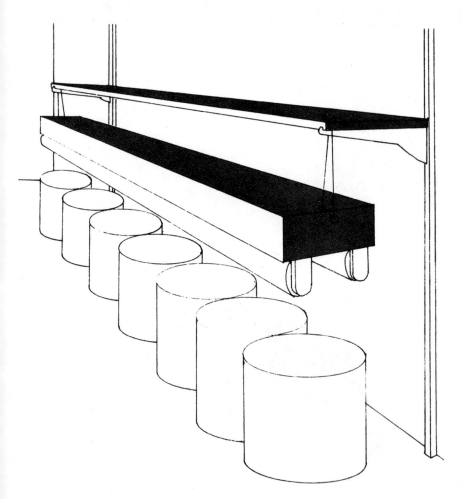

If you don't want to screw a bunch of hooks into your ceiling, you may want to buy some standards and brackets at a hardware store. I am referring to those used for making book shelves. The fixture can then be hung from the brackets. You will still have to drive a few screws into the wall, but this method works quite well because you can easily adjust the height of the brackets to raise the lights as the plants grow.

If you already have a book shelf, you can mount your fixture on the bottom part of each shelf and place your plants on the shelf below.

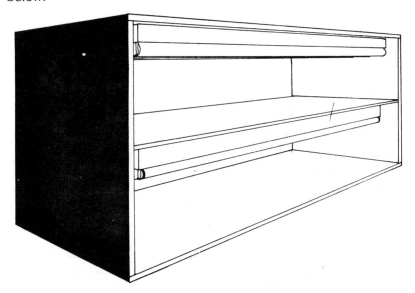

You will have to clip your plants often to keep them small, using this arrangement, but trimming them on a regular program (about every 10 days) will yield an amazing amount of foliage.

Another method is to make a frame to hold the lights.

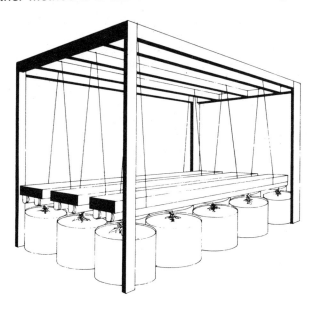

Appendix B
PROPAGATION TECHNIQUES

TAKING CUTTINGS

Taking cuttings (or "STARTS") off your marijuana plants enables you to have all female plants. You can also grow an entire new crop from your best female. You can choose the biggest and healthiest plant from your crop and take cuttings so that every one of your offspring plants will have the same genetic structure and will grow at the same rate as the parent plant. This will save you months if you plan to produce a superior strain of cannabis.

The procedure is not complicated and the results are well worth the effort.

To start new plants, warm a razor blade slightly (80 degrees F.) and cut off a branch at a 45 degree angle. Cut the stalk so that the cut off portion has about three sets of leaves on it. Set this new cutting in a Jiffy-7 container, or in a pot with sterilized soil. Dip the cutting in Rootone. Ideally these new cuttings should be in a humid atmosphere. By making a plastic tent around them you can crease a perfect environment for cuttings. Also an aquarium works very well.

Put either a piece of glass or clear plastic wrap over the top to retain the humidity.

A Gro-Lux light should be kept about 12 inches above the cuttings. They will take about three weeks to grow roots. At this time, plant your newly rooted cutting in a large container.

Another way to take cuttings is by air layering.

Cut a V-shaped incision into the stalk, being careful not to cut all the way through.

Cut a piece of cheese cloth about two inches by three inches. Put some peat moss or sphagnum moss on the cloth and dampen. Wrap the cheese cloth and the moss around the stlk at the V-shaped incision. With a string, loosely tie the top and bottom of the cheese cloth so that it is attached firmly to the stalk. In about 20 days roots will be growing into the peat moss from the incision, and you can then cut the stalk off just below the point where the cloth is wrapped.

Now plant the newly rooted cutting in soil. You may untie the cheesecloth but do not remove it if the roots are growing through because you may damage them. This cheesecloth will eventually disintegrate, so you need ot worry that the new roots will be confined.

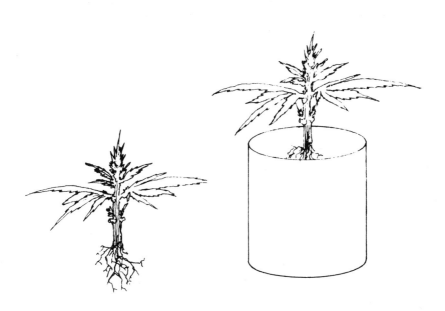

Appendix C
SUPPLIES CATALOG

Gro-Lux Lamps

18"	$ 3.50
24"	4.00
36"	4.00
48"	5.00
48" ws	2.25
48" VHO	8.50
48" VHO ws	7.00
*96"	6.10
*96" ws	3.75
*96" HO	7.50
*96" HO ws	4.00
*96" VHO	10.25
*96" VHO ws	6.75

Fixtures and Lamps

18" w/1 lamp	$12.00
24" w/1 lamp	14.00
24" w/2 lamps	21.00
36" w/1 lamp	14.00
48" w/1 std. lamp	15.00
48" w/1 std and 1 ws	26.00
48" w/hood	31.00
48" w/2 std lamps	27.50
48" VHO 1 std and 1 ws	75.00
48" VHO w/2 std	80.00
*96" 73 watt w/1 std and 1 ws	34.50
*96" 73 watt w/2 std lamps	38.00
*96" HO w/1 std and 1 ws	55.00
*96" HO w/2 std lamps	60.00
*96" VHO w/1 std and 1 ws	75.00
*96" VHO w/2 std lamps	80.00

Shipping Information: Please note that the following lamps cannot be shipped via U.P.S. or U.S. post office because of the length. Therefore it is necessary to ship via truck at a minimum rate of $18.00 for shipping and insurance for up to 100 lbs. delivered to your door. $10.00 for Washington, Oregon, and Idaho.

VITA-LITE: It is the closest thing to natural sunlight of any fluorescent lamps. Contains the same ultra-violet rays that the sun produces which is essential for animal health. It is recommended for environments where animals are kept and even for home lighting. Will fit normal fluorescent fixtures with Rapid-Start Ballasts.

24" (20 watt)	$ 6.15	24" fixture w/2 lamps $27.00
48" (40 watt)	6.39	48" fixture w/2 lamps 31.00
96" (75 watt)	12.58	96" fixture w/2 lamps 51.00

Please write or phone for information on 96" HO, 48" and 96' VHO lamps and fixtures.

Acidity Tester $2.75

Learn your lime requirements. "Liming and fertilizing without a soil test is like building a house without a blueprint." Easy to use pH tester with a list of acid preferences for lawn grasses, vegetables, fruits and flowers; complete instructions are enclosed.

Large $15.95
Medium, Size D .... $ 9.95

Tests pH, nitrogen, phosphorus, and potash content of soil.

Grow better plants with this complete kit. Tells you what to add to your soil for better plants. Complete instructions enclosed. It also comes with an organic supplement to let you know what natural elements will alter the chemistry of the soil.

Jiffy - 7

Peat pellets .... 59¢ dz.
(½ lb. per dozen)

These pellets when put in water expand to seven times their original size in about 5 minutes.

This is the best way of starting seedlings since the seeds grow fast and when the plants are about four inches high all you have to do is place the whole expanded pellet in the soil.

Jiffy Pots

3" diameter .... 59¢ dz.
2½" diameter .... 45¢ dz.
(½ lb. per dozen)

No transplanting problems with these either. They are basically the same as Jiffy -7's, except these are flower pots that are made of compressed peat moss. They decompose when transplanted into a larger container.

SUDBURY
Tailor-Made Fertilizers

These fertilizers along with the soil test kits also offered by Sudbury, will enable you to mix your plant nutrients to the exact specifications needed. For example, if your soil test color chart indicates your soil needs 4 percent nitrogen, 12 percent phosphorus, and 8 percent potash, you would mix 4 parts nitrogen (unit x) 12 parts phosphorus (unit y) and 8 parts potash (unit z), and dissolve 1 tablespoon of the mixture in a gallon of water and apply with a watering can.

Unit X, 44 percent nitrogen .... $2.29 ea.

Produces rich, luxuriant growth of stalks, stems, and leaves of plants and grasses. Stimulates green growth.

Unit Y, 44 percent phosphorus .... $2.29 ea.

Gives plant a rapid start, stimulates root formation, hastens maturity, aids blooming and seed formation. Most soils are **seriously** deficient in phosphorus.

Unit Z, 44 percent potash .... $2.29 ea.

Stimulates early root or tuber formation. Improves all underground vegetables or **tuberous** flowers.

FERTILIZERS

ALASKA FISH FERTILIZER

8 oz. $1.59
4 oz. 90

5 percent nitrogen
1 percent phosphorus
1 percent potash

A complete liquid plant food with trace elements. Derived from pure organic fish.

RA-PID-GRO

8 oz. $1.25
1 lb. $1.98

Used by experts since 1932.

Improved ROOTONE, 12 gm. . . . . .98¢
With fungicide to control damping-off. Stimulates development in cuttings.

TRANSPLANTONE, ½ oz. . . . . .59¢
Hormone-like starter for flowers and shrubs. Reduces wilt and loss when transplanting seedlings.

SPRAY BOTTLE

A spray bottle is an essential for foliar feeding your plants. Creates a fine mist. Is good for spraying water on leaves of ferns, philodendrons, and other plants that need high humidity.

1 quart cap $2.50
1 pint cap $1.59

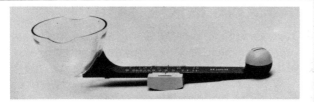

BALANCE SCALE

Large $14.95
Small 6.95

New! Of high impact plastic. Very accurate. Capacity of small, 125 grams; large, 500 grams.

COLCHICINE

Bulbs .... $2.50 ea.

This chemical causes mutations in plants. Caution should be taken since it is poisonous. The colchicine comes in its organic form, therefore it must be extracted from these special flower bulbs that contain .3 percent colchicine. The very easy process takes only minutes. One bulb is enough for many hundreds of plants. Makes polyploidal plants.

24 Hour Timers, ½ lb. $8.95
Sphagnum moss, 8 oz. dry 2.25
Black Magic, 5 oz. dry .... .59
African Violet Planting Mix
    Blossom Booster, 4 fl. oz. .... .79

MISCELLANEOUS

ORDERING INFORMATION

Minimum Orders are $5.00 plus $1.50 for postage and handling. If orders are over 3 lbs. enclose $1.00 only for handling plus the amount of the order and we will C.O.D. postage.

We accept C.O.D. orders with a 50 percent deposit. Prices are subject to change without notice.

Please specify   (1) Item Letter
                 (2) Quantity
                 (3) Price

SEND ORDERS TO:

Indoor Sun Sales
P.O. Box 33083 (7331)
Seattle, Washington 98133
Phone: (206) 365-8384